# EYE TO EYE WITH DOGS

# BULLDOGS

## Lynn M. Stone

Rourke
Publishing LLC
Vero Beach, Florida 32964

www.rourkepublishing.com

PHOTO CREDITS: All photos © Lynn M. Stone

Editor: Robert Stengard-Olliges

Cover and page design by Nicola Stratford

**Library of Congress Cataloging-in-Publication Data**

Stone, Lynn M.
  Bulldog / Lynn M. Stone.
    p. cm. -- (Eye to eye with dogs)
  Includes index.
  ISBN 1-60044-238-2 (hardcover)
  ISBN 978-1-60044-318-3 (paperback)
  1. Bulldog--Juvenile literature. I. Title. II. Series: Stone, Lynn M. Eye
to eye with dogs.
  SF429.B85S76 2007
  636.72--dc22
                                        2006010899

**Printed in the USA**

CG/CG

Rourke Publishing

www.rourkepublishing.com – sales@rourkepublishing.com
Post Office Box 3328, Vero Beach, FL 32964

# Table of Contents

*The bulldog has the most famous of dog faces.*

# The English Bulldog

The English bulldog's reputation for toughness and its wide, wrinkled face are famous. Who does not recognize those jaws and **jowls**?

Many schools have adopted the bulldog as their mascot. A diesel locomotive is called "bulldog" because of its broad, blunt nose. But are bulldogs really the tough guys they appear to be?

| BULLDOG FACTS |
|---|
| **Weight:** 40 – 60 pounds (18 – 27 kg) |
| **Height:** 12 – 15 inches (31 – 38 cm) |
| **Country of Origin:** England |
| **Life Span:** 8 – 10 years |

The first English bulldogs were strong, vicious dogs. They fought bulls in pits. Modern bulldogs look much like their ancestors, but they are not vicious. Instead, they are gentle, loveable companions. They are among the most mild-mannered dog **breeds**.

*A bulldog pup is more gentle than tough.*

*A bulldog enjoys a belly rub.*

# The Dog for You?

Bulldogs, wrinkles and all, are difficult not to like. They even greet strangers good-naturedly. They love attention and wag their tails – what little they have to wag – with great energy. A guard dog the bulldog is not.

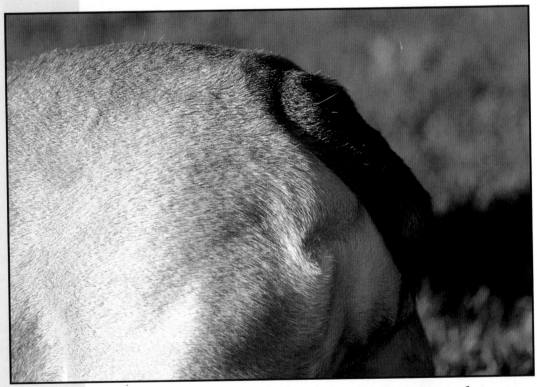

*A bulldog's tail is naturally short, but long enough to wag.*

*A bulldog steps out for a walk with its owner.*

Bulldogs need outdoor exercise, but not a great deal of exercise. They are neither distance runners nor swimmers.

*A bulldog bounds after a tennis ball.*

Many bulldogs can earn basic **agility**, tracking, or obedience titles. But bulldogs are more indoor than outdoor companions. They would like to be lap dogs, but the average bulldog weighs about 50 pounds (23 kg). That is more dog than most owners want on their laps!

Bulldogs have short coats, so they do not need constant brushing. Bulldog wrinkles require regular care so that they remain clean and free from infection.

# Bulldogs of the Past

We know little about the early ancestors of the bulldog. Some believe that the breed developed largely from **mastiffs** and terriers in England.

*Wrinkles need attention to keep them clean.*

As bull **baiters** long ago, fearless bulldogs bit onto the noses of tied-up bulls. Many believed that a bull's meat would taste better if the animal were first bloodied in a fight. Bull baiting in England became a sport for spectators and dog owners. They also watched bears fight bulldogs.

*Bulldogs wear a tight, short coat.*

*Bulldog pups grow up to weigh about 50 pounds.*

England stopped bull fighting in 1835. Now the main reason to raise bulldogs was gone. The bulldog breed began to disappear.

A few bulldog **breeders**, however, wanted to save the bulldog breed. Over the years, they chose less **aggressive** bulldogs to be parents. The result of their careful work is today's good-natured companion dog.

# Looks

A bulldog stands on short legs, just 12 to 15 inches (32 – 38 centimeters) tall. Its head and shoulders are large. It carries much of its weight in the forward part of its body, like a miniature bison.

*The modern bulldog is a mellow fellow.*

*Good-natured bulldog is a true companion dog.*

Bulldogs have small, floppy ears and naturally short, sometimes curly, tails.

Bulldogs can be all white or have, reddish, fawn-colored, or black markings on a white background. Some have faint striping in a pattern called **brindle**.

*Bulldogs are built low to the ground.*

*A bulldog pup requires an owner's time and attention.*

# A Note about Dogs

Puppies are cute and cuddly, but only after serious thought should anybody buy one. Puppies, after all, grow up.

Remember: A dog will require more than love and patience. It will need healthy food, exercise, grooming, medical care, and a warm, safe place to live.

A dog can be your best friend, but you need to be its best friend, too.

Choosing the right breed for you requires homework. For more information about buying and owning a dog, contact the American Kennel Club or the Canadian Kennel Club.

# Glossary

**aggressive** (uh GRESS siv)– wanting to attack or attacking

**agility** (uh JILL uh tee)– the ability to perform certain athletic tasks, such as leaping through a hoop

**baiter** (BAYT er) – an animal used by people to anger another animal into attacking it

**breed** (BREED) – a particular kind of domestic animal within a larger, closely related group such as the English bulldog breed within the dog group

**breeder** (BREE duhr) – one who keeps adult dogs and raises their pups, especially one who does so regularly and with great care

**brindle** (BRIN duhl) – a pattern in which vertical lines show in an animal's coat

**jowls** (JOULZ) – loose flesh about the cheeks and lower jaws

**mastiff** (MASS tif) – any one of several breeds of very large dogs with that name

# Index

## Further Reading

American Kennel Club. *The Complete Dog Book*.
   American Kennel Club, 2006.
Frisch, Joy. *Bulldogs*. Smart Apple Media, 2004.
Rayner, Matthew. *Dog*. Gareth Stevens Publishing, 2004.

## Website to Visit

American Kennel Club – http://www.akc.org
Bulldog Club of America – http://www.thebca.org
Canadian Kennel Club – http://www.ckc.ca

## About the Author

Lynn M. Stone is the author of more than 400 children's books. He is a
talented natural history photographer as well. Lynn, a former teacher,
travels worldwide to photograph wildlife in its natural habitat.